GREETINGS FROM Las Vegas

GREETINGS FROM Las Vegas

PETER MORUZZI

GIBBS SMITH
TO ENRICH AND INSPIRE HUMANKIND

First Edition
23 22 21 20 19   5 4 3 2 1

Text © 2019 Peter Moruzzi

All rights reserved. No part of this book may be reproduced by any means whatsoever without written permission from the publisher, except brief portions quoted for purpose of review.

Published by
Gibbs Smith
P.O. Box 667
Layton, Utah 84041

1.800.835.4993 orders
www.gibbs-smith.com

Designed by Kurt Wahlner
Printed and bound in China

Gibbs Smith books are printed on either recycled, 100% post-consumer waste, FSC-certified papers or on paper produced from sustainable PEFC-certified forest/controlled wood source. Learn more at www.pefc.org.

Library of Congress Cataloging-in-Publication Data
Names: Moruzzi, Peter, author.
Title: Greetings from Las Vegas / Peter Moruzzi.
Description: First edition. | Layton, Utah : Gibbs Smith, [2019]
Identifiers: LCCN 2018059062 | ISBN 9781423651765 (jacketless hardcover)
Subjects: LCSH: Las Vegas (Nev.)—History. | Las Vegas (Nev.)—Pictorial works.
Classification: LCC F849.L35 M678 2019 | DDC 979.3/135—dc23
LC record available at https://lccn.loc.gov/2018059062

All images from author Peter Moruzzi's collection except the following:

© J. Paul Getty Trust. Getty Research Institute, Los Angeles (2004.R.10), pages 144, 145.

Getty Images, pages 101 (photo by Bettmann), 113 (photo by Bob Willoughby).

Sven A. Kirsten Collection, pages 127 author photo, 128 (right), 130 (bottom left and right), 134 (bottom left).

Courtesy of the Library of Congress, pages 19 (top right), 80 (top left), 152 (left).

Los Angeles Public Library Photo Collection, page 30 (center).

Courtesy of the Neon Museum, pages 168 (facing far left, facing above, facing below), 171 (above).

Courtesy of the Nevada Preservation Foundation, pages 37 (top left, right, bottom left), 39 (right), 142 (right), 143 (left and right).

Courtney Newman Collection, page 114 (bottom left).

Chris Nichols Collection, pages 24 (top left and right), 33 (bottom right), 37 (center), 106, 107 (left), 157 (bottom right), 164 (left).

Scott Schell Collection, pages 126, 130 (top right), 131 (bottom), 134 (top), 135 (top right), 137 (right).

Jerry Stefani Collection, pages 13 (bottom), 116, 117 author photo, 118 (top left and right, bottom left and right), 120 (top left), 121 (left and right), 122 (right), 123 (top left).

Department of Special Research Collections, UCSB Library, University of California, Santa Barbara, page 136.

Special Collections and Archives, University Libraries, University of Nevada, Las Vegas, pages 10 (top left and top right), 11 (bottom left and bottom right), 21 (right), 24 (bottom), 43 (right), 58, 61, 62 (right), 63, 66 (top), 68 (top and bottom), 69 (top), 73 (left), 74 (right), 77 (bottom left), 78 (bottom left), 81 (bottom left), 89 (right), 114 (right), 140 (bottom right), 142 (left), 160 (left), 165 (bottom right), 172.

Courtesy of Western Resort Publications; photographs by Ferris H. Scott, pages 38, 42 (top left), 48 (top left), 54, 62 (bottom left), 79, 86 (bottom right), 131 (top right).

Contents

Introduction	7
Frontier Town	9
Fremont Street	14
The Birth of the Strip	23
Boomtown	35
Breaking the Color Barrier	59
Vegas and the Mob	65
Glitter Gulch	70
Las Vegas After Dark	90
The Rat Pack	111
Motel Paradise by Jerry Stefani	117
Tiki Vegas by Sven A. Kirsten	127
Vegas Modern	139
Swinging '60s and Beyond	155

above: Louis Prima and Keely Smith. Icons of the Vegas lounge act.

Introduction

The urge to gamble seems to be innate in humankind. Some are attracted because they think they're lucky, some because they welcome an evening's entertainment, and still others because they're addicts who simply can't help themselves. Regardless of the motivation, gamblers have sought out venues to satisfy their craving since the first pair of carved ivories was tossed.

During the first half of the twentieth century, laying a bet was strictly illegal in most of America except at regulated horse and dog tracks. Just as with the banning of alcohol in the 1920s, the prohibition of gambling resulted in an underground world of backroom poker games, slot machines, craps tables, and roulette wheels in cities and their environs throughout the United States. Ramshackle roadhouses, speakeasies, bars, nightclubs, hotels, and private homes hosted illegal betting parlors. And there were famous carpet joints—large upscale nightclubs with plush carpeting and backroom gambling—that catered to the well-to-do in the resort communities of Hot Springs, Arkansas; New York's Saratoga Springs; Palm Springs, California; and South Florida. And then, in 1931, Nevada legalized gambling. In just a few decades the dusty frontier town of Las Vegas would replace the backroom parlors as it blossomed into the casino, resort, and entertainment capital of the world.

In claiming its entertainment capital moniker, Las Vegas initially adopted the popular format of the nightclub, which was the center of social life for many Americans before the dominance of television, before a younger generation rejected their parent's entertainment venues as stuffy and passé, before the political and social upheavals of the 1960s, before rock and roll and touchless dancing in rowdy clubs replaced the sophistication of Sinatra and the bossa nova. But there would remain one last holdout, one last oasis where middle-aged men and women could embrace the spirit of the American nightclub for a few more years: Las Vegas.

Over the course of a human lifetime, Las Vegas transformed itself many times over. There was Old West Vegas of the '30s and '40s, Hollywood Nightclub and Country Club Vegas of the '50s, Rat Pack Vegas of the early '60s, Elvis/Liberace/Wayne Newton Vegas of the late '60s and early '70s, Corporate Vegas of the '70s and '80s, Steve Wynn themed megaresort, over-the-top Vegas of the '90s and 2000s, the "What Happens in Vegas, Stays in Vegas" Vegas of Mayor Oscar Goodman, and the EDM DJ pool party Vegas of the 2010s. What the future of Las Vegas holds will be exciting to witness.

Frontier Town

In 1905, the year that Las Vegas was founded, the townsite was a railroad stop on the transcontinental route from America's northeast to Los Angeles. A feverish land auction that same year established Fremont Street as the town's center—a modest commercial corridor extending east from the railroad station at Main Street. Las Vegas was not much different from other western frontier towns of the day, with its economy firmly tied to the presence of the railroad. And like other frontier towns, it had a red-light district, known as Block 16, of saloons, gambling houses, and brothels located just one block north of Fremont Street.

Las Vegas grew slowly through the 1920s. Fremont Street's commercial properties included a bank, bakery, cafés, groceries, a drugstore, laundry, post office, and general store. Its largest buildings were

FINEST DRINKS in TOWN

left: Faro Bank, or Faro, was the favorite game of the frontier. Gamblers loved it. The hands played fast. And it was simple to learn.

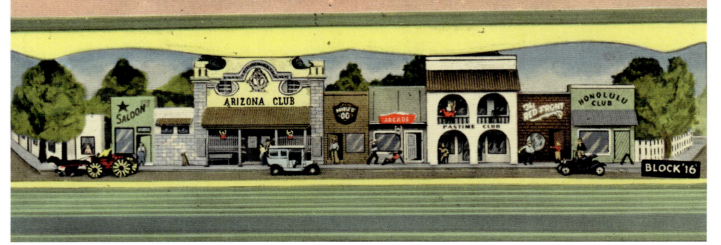

A DIORAMA OF FAMOUS BLOCK 16.

In 1905 when Las Vegas, Nevada was founded, this Block was reserved for Hotels, Bars and Restaurants. The early Day Trains stayed long enough in Las Vegas for the Passengers to walk there for a hot Meal or quick Drink. In later years it became quite Notorious, Catering to Men only until 1940.
No more Glamor or Excitement, today only Memories.

above left: Downtown circa 1909 with the original Union Pacific Railroad depot top center.

above right: Fremont Street circa 1910. A sleepy Western railroad town.

left: Block 16 was Las Vegas's "red light" district, just one block north of Fremont Street.

10 | GREETINGS FROM *Las Vegas*

the Overland and Nevada Hotels, situated across the street from each other on the corners of Main and Fremont opposite the Mission Revival–style railroad station. By 1930 there were also a few small clubs along Fremont Street, with saloons in the front and gambling rooms in the back. One of these was the Northern Club, whose proprietor, the legendary Mayme Stocker, managed the business with her two sons. Two events that would radically change the trajectory of Las Vegas were about to occur: the construction of Boulder Dam and Nevada's legalization of gambling.

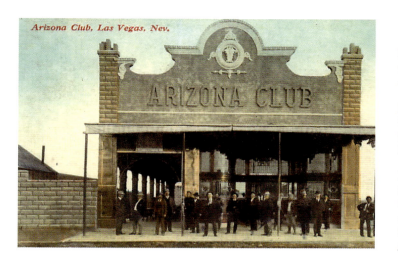

left: The Arizona Club circa 1906. One of the fancier saloons on Block 16.

below left: The Northern Club on Fremont Street in 1930, just before Nevada legalized gambling.

below right: Jovial Mayme Stocker was the Northern Club's proprietor. She would be the first person in Nevada to receive a gambling license in 1931.

FRONTIER TOWN | 11

In 1931, as the Great Depression deepened, the federal government began one of the most ambitious engineering projects ever conceived, the Boulder (later Hoover) Dam at the Arizona/Nevada border. To house the thousands of workers building the dam, a completely planned model city—Boulder City—was constructed nearby.

On March 19, 1931, desperate to stimulate its moribund economy, the Nevada legislature simultaneously legalized gambling and shortened the residency requirements for obtaining a divorce from three months to six weeks. As a result, up north, Reno became the "divorce capital of the world," with the city's casinos and showrooms entertaining divorcées-in-waiting to the benefit of the local economy. Unlike Reno, Nevada's largest city at the time, Las Vegas instead would focus on catering to the thousands of construction workers and their families living in Boulder City.

above: Construction began on the massive Boulder (later Hoover) Dam in 1931. It was completed in 1936.

left: The federal government built the sprawling Boulder City to house the dam's workers and families.

left: The "divorce trade" became an economic engine in Nevada, especially Reno, when residency requirements were reduced to only six weeks in 1931.

above: Fremont Street in the 1920s, before legalized gambling.

FRONTIER TOWN | 13

Fremont Street

The first to obtain a Clark County gambling license in 1931 was the Northern Club's Mayme Stocker. Other Fremont Street clubs soon followed, moving their backroom gambling tables to the front. On payday weekends, construction workers would trek the twenty-six miles from Boulder City to Fremont Street, filling the clubs to wager on poker games, roulette wheels, craps tables, and slot machines.

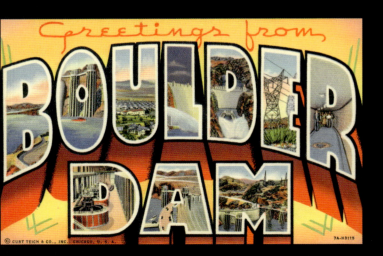

Along with Mayme Stocker, J. Kell Houssels Sr. was one of the early gaming pioneers, having secured a gambling license in 1931 for his Las Vegas Club on Fremont Street. He also was an investor in downtown's Boulder Club and later the

above: Boulder Dam near Las Vegas was a major tourist attraction.

facing: Fremont Street in 1943 during World War II.

above: Fremont Street in the early 1930s still had a cafe, shoe repair shop, liquor store, drugstore, and bank.

left: Can you spot the ladies wedged between the menfolk at the roulette table?

right: The Las Vegas Club opened in 1930.

El Cortez. On the Strip, Houssels would be one of the key backers of the Tropicana in the 1960s.

Tourism started becoming an important element of Las Vegas's economy as visitors arrived to witness the awe-inspiring construction of Boulder Dam. Many arrived via Highway 91, also known as the Los Angeles Highway, which reached Fremont Street in downtown Las Vegas.

The first visionary to recognize the vast potential of legalized gambling was former bootlegger Tony Cornero of Los Angeles. Selecting a site outside the Las Vegas city limits in unincorporated Clark County, Cornero and his brothers erected the Meadows in 1931. Unlike the Fremont Street clubs, the Meadows was a full-service resort hotel with supper club, sophisticated nightclub, and plush casino. Although destroyed by fire in 1936, the Meadows predicted the sprawling resorts of the Las Vegas Strip that would materialize in the following decade.

The Meadows was located just outside the city limits on the Boulder Highway. Operated by former bootlegger Tony Cornero and his brothers from 1931 to 1936, the Meadows was a full-service hotel with supper club, nightclub, and casino.

FREMONT STREET | 17

The Spanish-style El Cortez Hotel opened in November 1941, becoming the largest and most fashionable hotel-casino in the city. The property's Los Angeles–based developers—Marion B. Hicks and John C. Grayson—purposely chose a location three blocks east of the railroad station to distinguish their upscale operation from the crude gambling clubs along Fremont Street. Just one month after the El Cortez was completed, America entered World War II, the beginning of a five-year economic boom for Las Vegas as the US government invested millions in war-related facilities in the area.

In addition to a large military airbase, the massive Basic Magnesium, Inc. plant was constructed sixteen miles southeast of Las Vegas in what would become the town of Henderson. The lightweight metal magnesium was used for bomb casings and aircraft parts. In operation from 1940 through 1944, the company provided housing for 13,000 workers and their families, constituting 10 percent of Nevada's population. The war years helped prepare the region for the influx of tourism that would occur in the late 1940s as the Las Vegas Strip emerged as the key to the region's development.

facing: The full-service 1941 El Cortez was a major addition to Fremont Street.

above left: The sleek new Streamline Moderne–style Union Pacific Station replaced the original in 1940.

above right: During World War II, over 13,000 people were housed by Basic Magnesium, Inc. in what became the town of Henderson.

right: The Old West–themed Pioneer Club opened in 1942.

FREMONT STREET | 19

20 | GREETINGS FROM *Las Vegas*

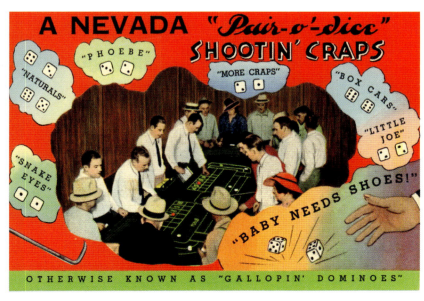

facing: Cornucopia of neon, 1942.

above: Tango was an early version of Keno.

below: Playing "Gallopin' Dominoes" because "Baby Needs Shoes!"

right: The Boulder Club was named in honor of the nearby dam.

FREMONT STREET | 21

The Birth of the Strip

EL RANCHO VEGAS

To set the record straight, the Las Vegas Strip was not the invention of gangster Benjamin "Bugsy" Siegel as he surveyed a desert wasteland along US Highway 91, the main route from Southern California, in 1946.

In fact, Chris Nichols—historian and biographer of architect Wayne McAllister—possesses concrete evidence showing that McAllister, San Diego investor Jack Barkley, and hotel man Thomas E. Hull had proposed an extravagant Spanish Colonial Revival–style resort-casino on Highway 91 as early as 1938. Its inspiration was the palatial Agua Caliente Casino and Hotel that McAllister had designed ten years earlier in Tijuana as a luxurious refuge from Prohibition for the

facing: A bevy of the El Rancho's long-legged lovelies.

Hollywood crowd. The group failed to entice additional investors, most likely because of the grand and costly nature of the project. However, Hull didn't give up on the concept, deciding instead to build a more modest Western-themed resort like the El Rancho properties he operated in Fresno and Sacramento. In 1941, on a parcel he had acquired just south of the Las Vegas city limits on Highway 91 where desert land was cheap and available, Hull commissioned McAllister to design El Rancho Vegas—a sprawling Western-themed hotel with a showroom, casino, swimming pool, sunning areas, and expansive lawns. The following year, in 1942, the Last Frontier hotel-casino, also Western-themed, appeared just down the road. Those two properties were the true genesis of the Las Vegas Strip.

above left: McAllister's unrealized 1938 concept for a luxurious Spanish-style resort to be built on what would become the Strip. **above right:** The architect's sumptuous Agua Caliente resort in Tijuana was the inspiration. **below:** Ultimately, Thomas Hull opted for a more modest Western-themed resort by McAllister, the El Rancho, instead. **facing:** The El Rancho's neon windmill became a beacon for weary motorists from Los Angeles.

THE BIRTH OF THE STRIP | 25

As architectural historian Alan Hess has meticulously documented, the original Strip resort properties were essentially glorified motels placed on the highway. Hess writes, "El Rancho set the pattern of the large highway resort hotel. With its opening, the builders of Las Vegas varied the motel archetype a bit: the sign was expanded, the lobby was enlarged to include a casino, and the room wings were surrounded by recreational facilities and lush planting. A bigger budget, a slightly different program but a motel nonetheless."

below: The El Rancho's Wild West gambling hall.

right: The new 1941 El Rancho as seen from the highway.

THE PIONEER LOBBY

HOTEL LAST FRONTIER
The Early West In Modern Splendor
Las Vegas, Nev.

LAST FRONTIER

Inspired by the apparent success of the El Rancho, Texas theater chain owner R. E. Griffith opened the Last Frontier just a mile down the road. Under the slogan "The Early West in Modern Splendor," the Last Frontier, like El Rancho, was designed in the rustic Ranch style. In this case, the Last Frontier took the theme much further when, in 1947, it re-created a small western village as a tourist attraction, featuring a saloon, jail, rooming house, gun shop, and steam locomotive with passenger cars.

above: Yellowstone's Old Faithful Inn was the inspiration for the Last Frontier's Pioneer Lobby.

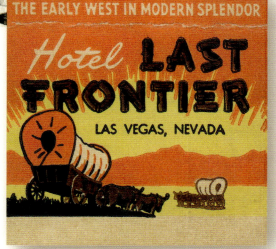

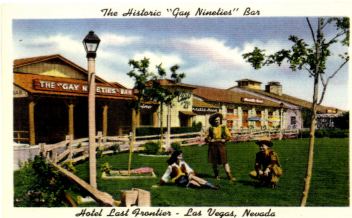

above: A magnificent neon sign announced Texaco's Fire Chief brand gasoline at the Last Frontier.

above right: Cowpokes on break from the Gay Nineties bar, 1940s.

facing: The Last Frontier's green lawn, umbrellas, and swimming pool beckon parched and weary travelers along the highway.

THE BIRTH OF THE STRIP | 29

Benjamin "Bugsy" Siegel took over the unfinished Flamingo from the financially strapped Billy Wilkerson in 1945.

FLAMINGO

In November 1945, Los Angeles nightclub and *The Hollywood Reporter* mogul Billy Wilkerson began construction of his Flamingo Hotel and Casino on the south end of Highway 91, which would soon be known as the Las Vegas Strip. Wilkerson hired Los Angeles architect George Vernon Russell, with the charge that he design a sophisticated desert version of the swank Ciro's and Trocadero nightclubs that Wilkerson owned on the Sunset Strip in Los Angeles. Specifically, the Flamingo was to be the complete opposite of the Old West–themed establishments then operating in Las Vegas.

Unfortunately, Wilkerson soon ran out of money due to the high cost of materials just after the war. Seeking financing, he accepted a large investment from a group headed by Harry Rothberg of New York—a group that Wilkerson would discover included mobsters Moe Sedway, Gus Greenbaum, Meyer Lansky, . . . and Benjamin "Bugsy" Siegel.

Siegel quickly recognized the brilliance of Wilkerson's vision. Pushing him aside, Siegel insisted upon a level of architectural refinement that far surpassed Wilkerson's original plans. That, paired with a mercurial tendency to demand expensive design changes, drove the project's cost far beyond its intended budget.

Rushing to finish before year's end, the Flamingo's hotel rooms were still not ready for guests at its December 26, 1946, opening. Without accommodations, customers took their winnings to properties up the road, resulting in huge losses for the new Flamingo and temporary closure. The cost overruns, fiasco of its grand opening, and behavior of

Casino and Restaurant, Hotel Flamingo, Las Vegas, Nevada

the uncontrollable Siegel were apparently too much for the project's other investors. Three months after the Flamingo's reopening in March 1947, Bugsy was shot dead as he sat reading the *Los Angeles Times* in the Beverly Hills living room of girlfriend Virginia Hill.

The new Flamingo Hotel and Casino of 1946 was patterned after the sleek, modern Sunset Strip nightclubs frequented by Bugsy Siegel and his Hollywood pals.

Management of the Flamingo immediately passed to Siegel colleagues Moe Sedway and Gus Greenbaum, who stabilized the property's finances. Ironically, soon after Bugsy's elimination, the chic Hollywood crowd that he had envisioned was packing the Flamingo every weekend. In just a few years, inspired by the astonishing success of the Flamingo, other mob-connected hotel-casinos appeared along the Las Vegas Strip, including the Desert Inn, Sahara, and Sands.

left: The Flamingo's chic casino outshone all others in sophistication upon opening in December 1946.

above: Relaxing poolside. Note Bugsy's penthouse suite atop the hotel.

THE BIRTH OF THE STRIP | 33

Boomtown

THUNDERBIRD

The next property to be built on the Strip, the Thunderbird of 1948, was a hybrid of the El Rancho's and Last Frontier's Old West theme and the Flamingo's Hollywood sophistication. Its most distinctive element was an enormous multicolored neon Thunderbird perched atop the hotel's central tower.

facing: Giant neon thunderbirds announced the arrival of the latest addition to the Strip.

The Desert Inn of 1950 was a refined synthesis of the Western Ranch style and contemporary flair.

DESERT INN

Around the time that Billy Wilkerson was planning his Flamingo project, San Diegan Wilbur Clark arranged financing for his dream project, the Desert Inn. Based upon an initial design by architect Wayne McAllister, foundations had been poured when Clark—like Wilkerson—ran out of money.

To his rescue came Morris "Moe" Dalitz and his underworld associates from Ohio. Unlike Wilkerson, Clark was fully aware of who he was dealing with, ceding majority control to Dalitz while keeping his name on the marquee. Wilbur Clark's Desert Inn opened in 1950 with a design by local architect Hugh Taylor. Not quite as stylistically modern as the Flamingo, the Desert Inn nonetheless was a refined synthesis of the Western Ranch style and contemporary flair. Topping the main building near its beautiful curvilinear neon sign was the Sky Room, a glass-enclosed lounge with spectacular views of the surrounding desert and mountains.

above left: Moe Dalitz was the man behind the curtain.

left: Wilbur Clark (left) and associate survey the project site.

above: The charming and dapper Wilbur Clark was the public face of the Desert Inn.

BOOMTOWN | 37

38 | GREETINGS FROM *Las Vegas*

left: Mr. Popular shows off to his gal friends.

right: The Desert Inn's glass-enclosed Sky Room cocktail lounge afforded a panoramic view of the surrounding desert.

above: Arriving in style at the new Sahara.

SAHARA

The Sahara was another hybrid, a Moroccan–Ranch Modern design with plaster desert nomads and camels near the highway. It opened in 1952. Undoubtedly the Sahara's lasting contribution to the identity of Las Vegas was its pioneering role in popularizing the Vegas lounge act when it booked Louis Prima and Keely Smith to perform in the casino's Casbar lounge in 1954.

left: Louis Prima and Keely Smith were pioneers in popularizing the Vegas lounge act. **above:** This camel caravan is here to see Louis and Keely perform in the lounge. **below:** The exotic Morocco Suite at the Sahara.

BOOMTOWN | 41

above: On the front lawn sketching the magnificent Sands sign.

above right: A white Cadillac convertible glides to a stop beneath the porte cochere's dramatic doglegs.

right: A rare front view of the Sands's ultra-modern entrance.

facing: A gimmicky but fun 1954 publicity shot of a "floating craps game" in the Sands pool.

SANDS

Architect Wayne McAllister was responsible for the 1952 Sands design, which was influenced by the Late Moderne style that he and partner William Wagner were applying to restaurants in Los Angeles. The Sands's triangular porte cochere supported by a trio of massive doglegs, as well as the full-height plate glass entrance, distinguished the building as cutting-edge modern.

McAllister's design for the Sands sign was itself a monumental work of art. Fabricated by the Young Electric Sign Company (YESCO), it was fifty-six feet tall with an eggcrate grid projecting from and above a soaring pylon. On both sides, rendered in elegant script, was the word *Sands*. The neon *S* was thirty-five feet tall, with *ands* ranging in height from six to fourteen feet. The sophisticated slogan "A PLACE IN THE SUN" floated from the grid and pylon.

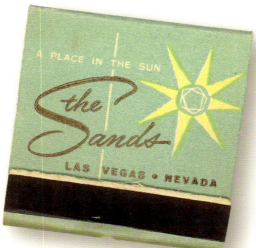

FLAMINGO

Only six years had passed between the Flamingo's opening and the completion of the Sands, yet the Flamingo was already dated in its restrained appearance and modest scale. The Flamingo's extensive 1953 remodel by Pereira and Luckman of Los Angeles defiantly challenged the Sands in upscale modernity.

above: The Flamingo's flashy 1953 remodel radiated midcentury luxury.

facing: The Flamingo's fabulous champagne tower was a soaring beacon of bubbles on the Strip.

44 | GREETINGS FROM *Las Vegas*

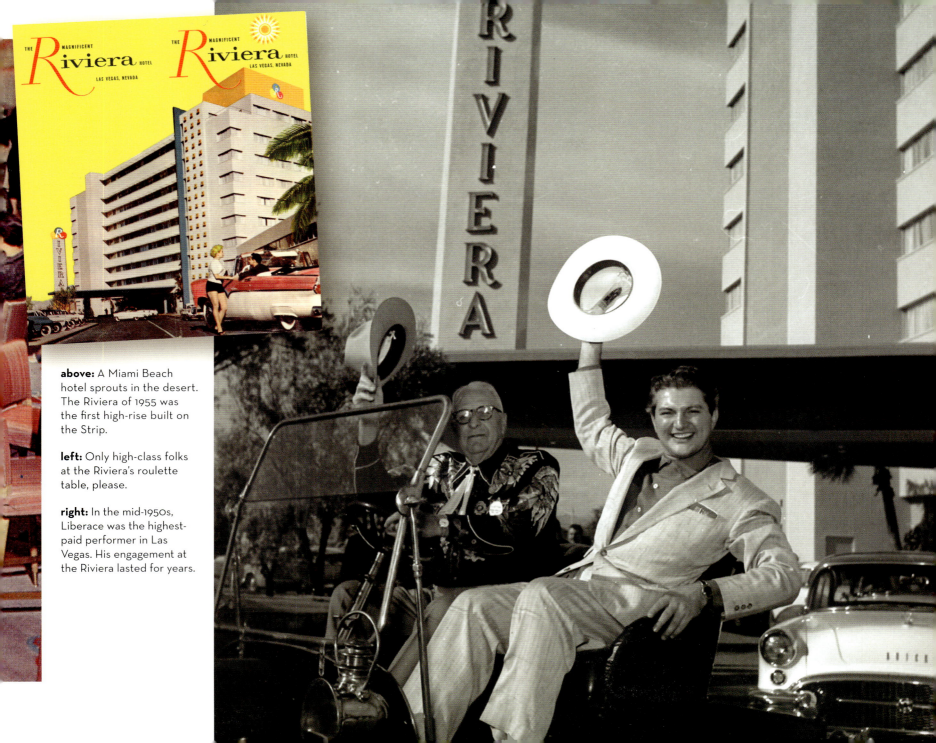

above: A Miami Beach hotel sprouts in the desert. The Riviera of 1955 was the first high-rise built on the Strip.

left: Only high-class folks at the Riviera's roulette table, please.

right: In the mid-1950s, Liberace was the highest-paid performer in Las Vegas. His engagement at the Riviera lasted for years.

above: The New Frontier jettisoned its Old West heritage for sleek modernism in 1955.

right: The 1955 Royal Nevada was absorbed by the adjacent Stardust in 1959.

facing: A 35-foot fiberglass sultan atop his nomadic tent greets guests at the 1955 Dunes.

Royal Nevada Hotel
Las Vegas, Nevada

48

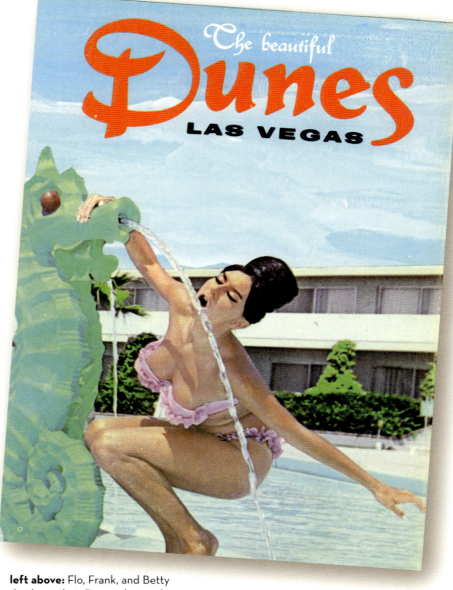

left above: Flo, Frank, and Betty divide up their Dunes slot machine winnings.

left: Doris mirrors the Sultan's pose in demonstrating how he would look in a sweater and skirt.

above: Who came up with this concept for the promo brochure?

facing: The Tropicana billed itself as "the Tiffany of the Strip" when it opened in 1957. Unfortunately, Edsel was the Kmart of American cars.

BOOMTOWN | 51

TONY CORNERO'S STARDUST

Former bootlegger Tony Cornero and his brothers operated the Meadows resort hotel-casino just outside the Las Vegas city limits from 1931 until its loss by fire in 1936 (see page 17). Two years later, in 1938, Cornero launched the S.S. Rex, one of several notorious gambling boats that operated just beyond the California coastline's three-mile jurisdictional limit. Water taxis ferried customers for twelve-minute rides to Cornero's round-the-clock floating casino "anchored in calm waters off Santa Monica Pier." The S.S. Rex and a handful of other gambling boats operated until 1939, when the authorities raided the ships and tossed the slot machines and other gambling equipment overboard.

Undeterred, Cornero relocated to Las Vegas in 1945 to open a small casino he named the S.S. Rex Club in downtown's Apache Hotel (see page 80). Unfortunately for Cornero, he was denied a gambling license and his club closed soon after. Following another attempt at reviving offshore gambling just after World War II, Tony Cornero made his last stand in Las Vegas with his dream project, the Stardust.

above: Tony Cornero had two previous forays in Las Vegas—the Meadows (1931–36) and the S.S. Rex Club (1945). The Stardust would be his last stand in the Nevada desert.

left: Cornero's S.S. Rex gambling boat operated off Santa Monica from 1938 to 1939 before being raided by the authorities and shut down.

52 | GREETINGS FROM *Las Vegas*

left: Cornero named his Fremont Street club after his former gambling boat, the S.S. *Rex*. It lasted less than one year.

right: The dazzling Stardust was Tony Cornero's dream project. It broke ground in early 1955. Cornero died at the Desert Inn's craps table a few months later.

below: Poolside at the Stardust.

BOOMTOWN | 53

above: The Stardust was known for its over-the-top shows.

Cornero's final investment was based on his awareness from operating gambling boats that ordinary middle-class folks were a much larger potential market than the high rollers and country club regulars particular to the Flamingo, Desert Inn, and Sands. This insight guided his vision of a massive resort-casino on the Las Vegas Strip—Tony Cornero's Stardust—that would cater to the average Joe and Janet with the formula of clean, comfortable, budget-priced rooms, modestly priced restaurants, and over-the-top popular entertainment.

Cornero spent 1954 raising funds for his Stardust project, which broke ground in 1955. Then, on July 31, 1955, Tony Cornero "died of coronary thrombosis after a night-long session at the dice tables at the Desert Inn. Companions said that he was behind $10,000 and was 'trying to get even,'" according to the *Los Angeles Times*.

right above: The former Royal Nevada (left) became the Stardust Auditorium. At the center is the Aku Aku Polynesian restaurant. The sprawling Stardust is on the right.

right: The parallel rows of Stardust motel rooms recall railroad boxcars.

BOOMTOWN | 55

Tony Cornero's untimely death left the Stardust unfinished for two years, until new investors led by Moe Dalitz of the Desert Inn took over. When completed in 1958, there were five rows of two-story motel rooms stretching west behind the enormous 16,500-square-foot casino, massive showroom, restaurant space, and swimming pool. Covering the facade of the plain, warehouse-like building was a space age solar system of planets and stars with a colossal globe of Earth in the center ringed by a satellite. At 216 feet wide, the Stardust sign was the largest on the Strip, ushering in a new wave of bigger-is-better sign competition that lasts to this day.

left: Artist Kermit Wayne of the Young Electric Sign Company (YESCO) designed the colossal Stardust sign, the widest on the Strip at 216 feet.

BOOMTOWN | 57

Breaking the Color Barrier

Since the 1940s, African Americans had been major marquee stars at all of the Las Vegas hotels, yet they were generally not permitted to stay where they performed. Neither were African Americans welcomed on the casino floors or as guests in the showrooms. Recognizing a market opportunity, in 1955 three white entrepreneurs opened the Moulin Rouge as Las Vegas's first integrated hotel-casino. It was located on Bonanza Road in the western part of the city, well away from Fremont Street and the Strip. Promotions for the Moulin Rouge boasted that it "is renowned as the first truly cosmopolitan hotel in this famous resort city. The Moulin Rouge is a new world of luxury, sport, and fun."

facing: Moulin Rouge showgirl 1955.

Almost immediately the property became a late-night hangout for famous African American stars and well-known white performers, who would drop by the Moulin Rouge after their shows at other venues ended at 2 a.m. Many headlined there.

The Moulin Rouge also became a gathering place for Vegas's large African American community. Special events were celebrated in the hotel's banquet rooms, showroom, lounge, and bars. It was a terrible shock when the Moulin Rouge suddenly shut its doors without warning only six months after its celebrated opening. It's not entirely clear what caused the property's failure. Whether it closed due to mismanagement or was driven out of business by the owners of the big Strip casinos upset by the competition is unknown. Yet the fact of the Moulin

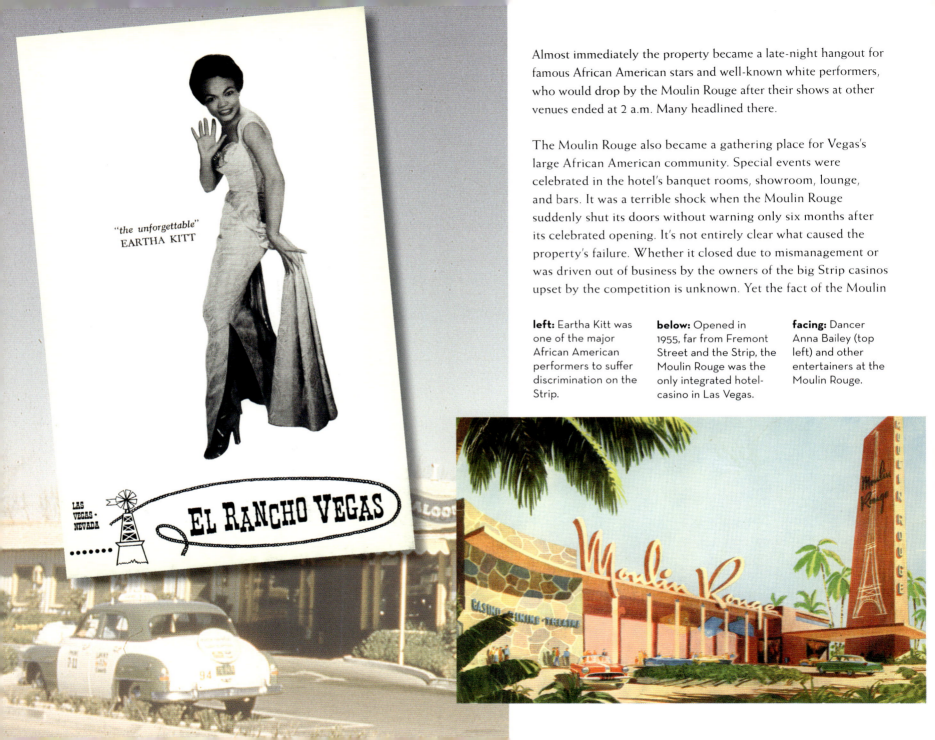

left: Eartha Kitt was one of the major African American performers to suffer discrimination on the Strip.

below: Opened in 1955, far from Fremont Street and the Strip, the Moulin Rouge was the only integrated hotel-casino in Las Vegas.

facing: Dancer Anna Bailey (top left) and other entertainers at the Moulin Rouge.

BREAKING THE COLOR BARRIER | 61

Rouge's brief existence created new momentum in fighting Las Vegas's blatant segregation.

In 1960, inspired by nationwide demonstrations and fed up with the status quo, the local chapter of the NAACP announced it would stage a protest march on the Las Vegas Strip. Alarmed about the negative publicity, the casino owners tacitly supported a meeting of African American community leaders, elected officials, and local newspaper publisher Hank Greenspun to reach a verbal agreement integrating Las Vegas. The meeting was held at the closed Moulin Rouge. Although gaining full civil rights for Las Vegas's African American community would take at least another decade, the 1960 agreement was a key milestone in that effort.

below: Despite its popularity, the resort closed within 6 months for unexplained reasons.

right: Jazz musician and bandleader Lionel Hampton (far left) with Moulin Rouge performers.

facing: City officials and NAACP members meet in 1960 at the closed Moulin Rouge to end segregation on the Las Vegas Strip.

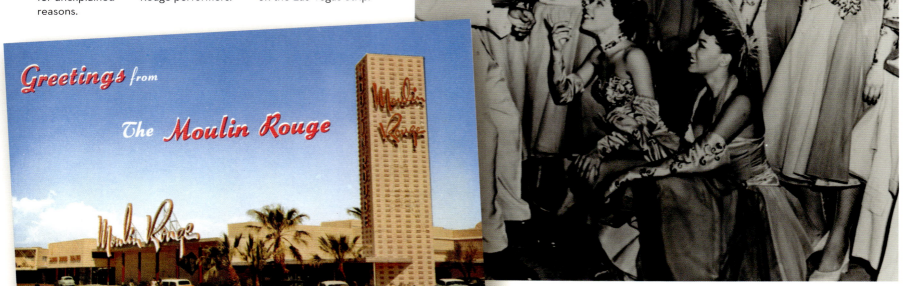

62 | GREETINGS FROM *Las Vegas*

Vegas and the Mob

The gambling business has always attracted a colorful collection of characters, many with shady backgrounds linked to bootlegging, bookmaking, and illegal backroom wagering. When the Nevada legislature legalized gambling in 1931, an opportunity for experienced gaming operators—and a chance to go legit—suddenly emerged. Some of these entrepreneurs began by investing in the small Fremont Street clubs, including A. T. McCarter at the Exchange Club and J. Kell Houssels Sr. at the Las Vegas Club. In the late 1930s, representatives from the bigger Midwest and East Coast syndicates arrived to partake in the action, including Moe Sedway and Bugsy Siegel. In 1945, Sedway and his partners bought the El Cortez, then sold it the following year to invest in a much more significant project—the Flamingo.

facing: The busy El Cortez casino. From 1945–46, a mob syndicate owned the property.

right: The Desert Inn's Moe Dalitz (left), Wilbur Clark (second from right), and Toni Clark with Elvis and Juliet Prowse on the Hollywood set of *G.I. Blues*.

below: Riviera investors "Ice Pick Willie" Alderman, Dave Berman, and Joe "Bowser" Rosenberg.

Wish You Were Here!

The 1950s boom of the Las Vegas Strip was assisted by the active involvement of mob-connected newcomers of varying degrees of notoriety, such as Moe Sedway and Gus Greenbaum (El Cortez, Flamingo), Moe Dalitz (Desert Inn, Stardust), "Ice Pick Willie" Alderman (Riviera), and Tony Cornero (Stardust). Others, like Benny Binion (Horseshoe), were convicted outlaws without archetypal Italian or Jewish roots.

In the ensuing decades, some of these fellows became leading businessmen and philanthropists who helped to build the modern Las Vegas. Chief among them was Moe Dalitz, also known as Mr. Las Vegas. Among his causes were obtaining land, buildings, and furnishings for the University of Nevada, Las Vegas, and helping to build the Las Vegas Convention Center, Sunrise Hospital, and Las Vegas Country Club.

CASE STUDY:
EL CORTEZ, BUGSY, MEYER, AND MOE

On March 28, 1945, a story appeared in the *Las Vegas Review-Journal* that would henceforth link the El Cortez to some of America's most notorious underworld figures. Under the headline "El Cortez Sold," the newspaper reported that the buyers were Edward Berman of Minneapolis and Moe Sedway of Las Vegas, with a purchase price of $800,000. Conveniently, perhaps for tax purposes, the actual deed officially recorded on April 6, 1945, stated that the purchase price was, farcically, $10.

New owner Moe Sedway, who hailed from New York, was a longtime associate of high-profile gangsters Meyer Lansky and Bugsy Siegel. Sedway had arrived in Las Vegas earlier in 1941 to partake in the city's growing gambling business. Colleague Edward Berman was a Minnesota crime figure who had just relocated to the desert city. Yet, just eight months later, the *Las Vegas Review-Journal* reported another ownership change. Moe Sedway would partner with an investment syndicate headed by Gus Greenbaum—a known underworld figure—along with "other members [who] were not revealed by Sedway," according to the newspaper. Who were the "other members"? Meyer Lansky and Bugsy Siegel.

The new investment syndicate didn't hold the El Cortez for long, selling their holdings to J. Kell Houssels Sr. (investor in Fremont Street's Boulder Club) and Raymond R. Salmon just eight months later. In all, Moe Sedway and his various associates owned the El Cortez for only seventeen months. Why? Their cash was needed for a much bigger project rising from the desert on the Los Angeles Highway—the Flamingo.

above: Moe Sedway and Gus Greenbaum at the Flamingo Hotel in 1948, following their sale of the El Cortez.

VEGAS AND THE MOB | 67

BENJAMIN "BUGSY" SIEGEL

The life of Bugsy Siegel has been mythologized in newspapers, books, television, and movies. A feared member of New York's Lucky Luciano crime syndicate, Siegel was known for his quick and violent temper. His connection to Las Vegas began in the early 1940s, when he and mob associate Moe Sedway invested in the Northern Club on Fremont Street. This was part of the syndicate's expansion of its Trans-America Race Wire Service, as it attempted to take business from an already established competitor. Utilized by bookies and casinos, the race wire was an invaluable network of telegraph wires that provided instant horse racing results from tracks across the country. Siegel would become involved with Fremont Street's El Cortez in 1945, and most notably the Flamingo starting in 1946 (see page 30).

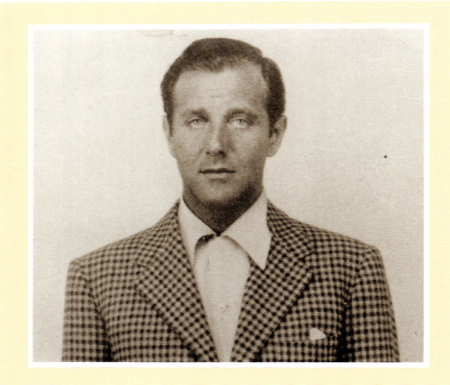

The sale of the Desert Inn by Moe Dalitz to reclusive billionaire Howard Hughes in 1967 was the beginning of the corporatization of the Strip and the decline of mob involvement. By 1980, the transition was complete and bland conformity enshrined. Then, starting with the Mirage in 1989, real estate mogul Steve Wynn revived the era of entrepreneurial visionaries who shaped Las Vegas in its formative years.

right: Chicago Outfit enforcer Anthony "Tony the Ant" Spilotro (left) with mob lawyer Oscar Goodman in 1980. Goodman would later become the popular mayor of Las Vegas most associated with the slogan "What Happens in Vegas, Stays in Vegas."

above: In 1962, Catholic dignitaries celebrate the groundbreaking of Las Vegas's Guardian Angel Cathedral on the Strip. Local casino notables who raised funds for the cathedral include Gus Greenbaum (second from left), "Ice Pick Willie" Alderman (sixth from left), and Benny Binion (third from right). The cathedral opened in 1963.

left: Many of the Guardian Angel Cathedral's stained glass windows, this one featuring Vegas Strip properties, were sponsored by Wilbur Clark and other casino luminaries.

VEGAS AND THE MOB | 69

Gulch casinos expanded by taking over adjacent commercial spaces, including a number of the original gambling clubs.

As the Strip resorts multiplied, Fremont Street attempted to keep up by adding bigger signs with more neon. Among the earliest companies responsible for creating the signs was the Young Electric Sign Company (YESCO) of Salt Lake City, which would

above: The Golden Nugget featured a gold rush–era Barbary Coast theme.

right: The first Las Vegas sign designed by the Young Electric Sign Company (YESCO) was for the Boulder Club; the Golden Nugget was its second. Both were erected in 1946.

The Las Vegas Club sign by YESCO was four times the height of the building.

soon dominate the field. YESCO's first commission was for the Boulder Club in 1946, with a large, streamlined, vertical blade sign that was more modern than Old West (see page 21). That same year the Golden Nugget opened with a YESCO sign evocative of San Francisco's Barbary Coast during the gold rush (see previous pages). Rising to the occasion, in 1949 the Las Vegas Club commissioned YESCO to design a soaring vertical sign four times the height of the building.

above: Relaxing atop the Las Vegas Club sign with a Coke and a smile.

right: With their frontages open to the sidewalk, the Glitter Gulch casinos created an informal intimacy with the street that the Strip casinos couldn't match. Looking west (above), and looking east (below).

GLITTER GULCH | 73

The city's chamber of commerce introduced Vegas Vic to the world in 1947. He would appear in ads, brochures, and billboards through the 1950s. However, Vic's greatest incarnation was as the fifty-foot mascot for the Pioneer Club when he rose from the building in 1951. Designed by YESCO, the neon Vic's animated sheet-metal arms and hands gestured toward the gambling hall while his recorded voice announced "Howdy Podner" to the folks below every fifteen minutes.

below: The Las Vegas mascot Vegas Vic was introduced in 1947, appearing in ads, brochures, and billboards for many years.

right: YESCO's final sketch of Vegas Vic.

facing: Vegas Vic on duty at the Pioneer Club.

74 | GREETINGS FROM *Las Vegas*

When the Fremont Hotel was built, in 1956, it made a complete break from the Old West theme to embrace Midcentury Modernism. Designed by Wayne McAllister and William Wagner of Los Angeles, the thirteen-story Fremont Hotel, with pool and showrooms, was the state's tallest building at the time. Two years later, Las Vegas–based architects Walter Zick and Harris Sharp conceived of the radical Mint sign that covered the entire hundred-foot facade of the casino. Fabricated by YESCO in 1957, the sparkling lights of the Mint sign began on the sidewalk, pierced the undulating sidewalk canopy, curved up, down, then soared up again seventy feet to an exploding six-pointed star.

left: The Modern 1956 Fremont was a complete break from the Old West theme of Glitter Gulch.

below: The dazzling Mint sign was a soaring beacon of pink neon capped by an exploding star.

76 | GREETINGS FROM *Las Vegas*

Upon Benny Binion's return from a Texas prison in 1957, he took back control of the Horseshoe from Joe W. Brown, to whom he'd sold it before going off to jail. A few years later, Binion—ever the flamboyant entrepreneur—embarked on a spectacular physical makeover of his property. Cocoon is the only term to describe the cascade of aqua blue and white neon that encased the three-story Apache Hotel's exterior. When completed, the entire block from the Mint to the Horseshoe was one solid expanse of blazing neon. It was the apex of Glitter Gulch as the pictorial representation of Las Vegas. Unfortunately in the coming years, Fremont Street, hemmed in by its downtown location, would struggle in competition with the ever-expanding resorts along the Strip.

left: Fresh from prison, the flamboyant Texan Benny Binion took back control of the Horseshoe in 1957.

below left: Binion cocooned the old Apache Hotel in a cascade of blue and white neon.

facing: The newly encased Horseshoe glows at sundown.

78 | GREETINGS FROM *Las Vegas*

GLITTER GULCH | 79

1932

1941

APACHE HOTEL

The history of the Apache Hotel is an extraordinary example of how rapidly casino ownership changed downtown. A ground floor cafe faced Fremont Street when the Apache opened in 1932. Soon after, the Apache Casino would share the ground floor, lasting until 1940. It was the New Western Casino from 1941 to 1942, the S.S. Rex Club in 1945, the Rex Club in 1946, the Eldorado Club from 1947 to 1951, the Horseshoe from 1951 to 1953, Joe W. Brown's Horseshoe from 1953 to 1958, Binion's Horseshoe from 1958 to 2005, and since 2005 it's been known as Binion's Gambling Hall.

1945

1947

1951

1953

1958

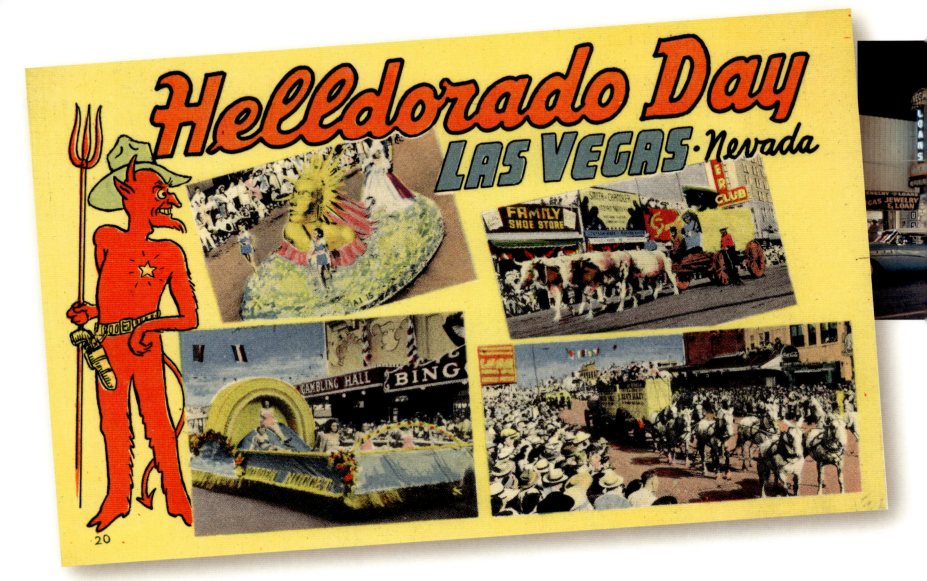

above: Helldorado is a rodeo, parade, and carnival organized by the local Elks Club that started in 1934. It lasted until 1998, resuming in 2005 as part of the city's centennial celebration.

opposite, clockwise from upper left: The Silver Palace lasted from 1956 until 1964, when it became the Carousel. Biff's Famous Food circa 1963. Butch playing the nickel slots in 1962, happy as a clam.

above: Fred and Madge at the Nevada Club, 1957.

left: Glamorous Barbara, 1960.

facing: Nancy and Walter, serious about their Lady Luck winnings.

below: Lucky Strike Club circa 1955.

right: One-armed bandits guard the entrance at the Las Vegas Club, "The House of Jackpots."

below right: Gettin' fresh with the Mint's one-armed bandit.

facing: YESCO's Kermit Wayne redesigned the Golden Nugget signage in 1957. Suddenly, the prominent corner was ablaze in gold neon—the sign as architecture.

86 | GREETINGS FROM *Las Vegas*

88 | GREETINGS FROM *Las Vegas*

An unexpected tourist attraction first appeared in the desert sky in 1951: the detonation of an atomic bomb at the Nevada Test Site, seventy-five miles northwest of Las Vegas. Fremont Street hotels promoted the regularly scheduled explosions over the next eleven years with viewing parties and atomic-themed cocktails. The aboveground nuclear tests continued until 1962.

facing: The "Up and Atom" city beckons. "Wish you were here!"

above: Benny Binion presents the many moods of the atom bomb.

right: Miss Atomic Bomb, Lee Merlin (Sands Copa Room showgirl), explodes with joy in 1957. What fun!

Las Vegas After Dark

People come to Las Vegas to gamble, but also to be entertained. In the 1950s it took the exceptional talents of impresarios such as the Sands's Jack Entratter and Bill Miller of the Sahara to set Las Vegas on the path to becoming the "Entertainment Capital of the World."

Jack Entratter hailed from New York as a co-owner of the famed Copacabana nightclub, where over the years he had booked the biggest names in show business. Starting in 1952, as the Sands's entertainment director, Entratter's connections brought America's top performers to the hotel's Copa Room, helping turn Las Vegas into the highest-paying venue for performers in the country. On the Sands's Copa stage appeared Louis Armstrong, Frank Sinatra, Lena Horne, Nat King Cole, Dean Martin,

facing: The New Frontier's Venus Room presents a Polynesian spectacular to a sellout crowd.

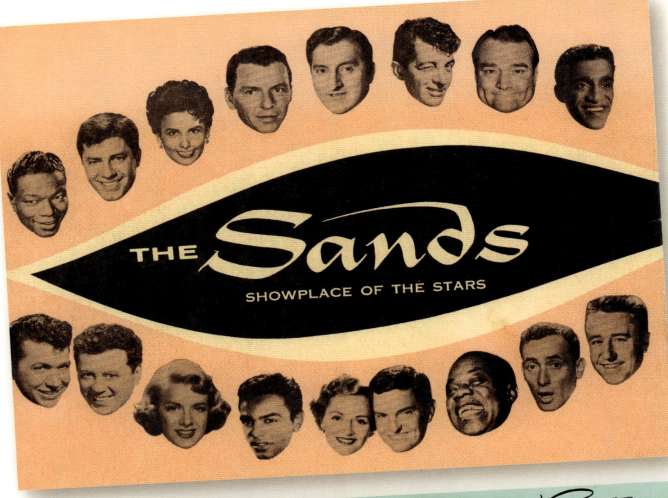

Rosemary Clooney, Eydie Gormé and Steve Lawrence, Jerry Lewis, the Will Mastin Trio with Sammy Davis Jr., Red Skelton, Johnny Mathis, and so many others.

Bill Miller was another East Coast transplant. His renowned cliffside Riviera nightclub in Fort Lee, New Jersey—with its hidden upstairs gambling parlor—had closed in 1953. That same year Miller relocated to Las Vegas to take over as the Sahara's entertainment director. It was there that Miller nurtured the emerging Vegas lounge act.

above left: Jack Entratter booked the biggest names in show business for the Sands's Copa Room.

below left: Sammy Davis Jr., performs with the Will Mastin Trio at the Sands. The trio included his father, Sammy Davis Sr.

facing: A bit long in the tooth by 1954, Mae West nonetheless starred in her own bawdy Las Vegas show at the Sahara. *Cabaret* magazine extolled, "Fabulous Siren Launches Comeback Making Mass Love to Harem of Huskies and Selling Sex Like Sixty—Which is Her True Age."

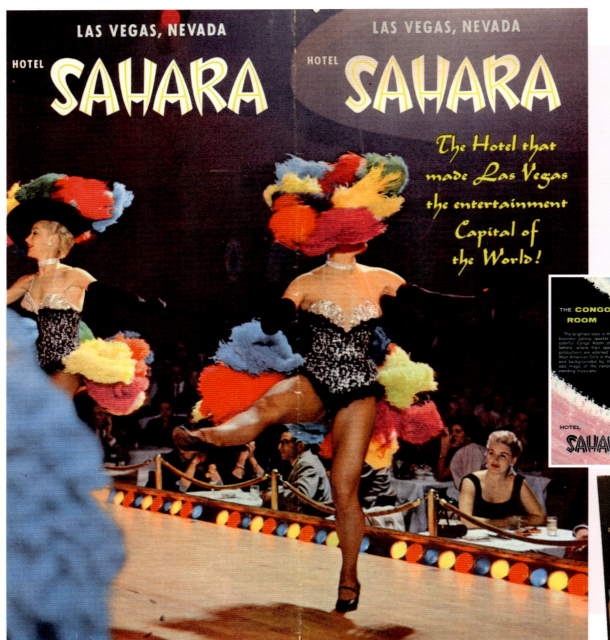

The Sahara's Congo Room theater restaurant was "Home of the most American Girls in the world." Whatever that meant.

94 | GREETINGS FROM *Las Vegas*

In a never-ending race to outdo each other, the Strip's hotels added more rooms, enlarged their casinos, and opened bigger showrooms. Star performers would appear for five days at the Sands's Copa Room, then a few weeks later turn up at the Sahara's Congo Room, followed by a run at the Stardust's Café Continental, or the Crystal Room at the Desert Inn. There were also the Tropicana's Blue Room, the New Frontier's Venus Room, and later in the 1960s, the Circus Maximus at Caesars Palace.

below: The Stardust's Café Continental featured a multitiered theatrical extravaganza.

INVENTING THE LAS VEGAS LOUNGE ACT

The pioneers of the Vegas lounge act were the dynamic Mary Kaye Trio at the Last Frontier. They performed on a small bar stage near the casino floor with a high-energy show that had the magical effect of keeping gamblers at the tables into the wee small hours of the morning.

In November 1954, a broke and desperate Louis Prima—one-time New Orleans big band leader—called Bill Miller from New York asking if he would hire Prima's five-member musical group for a gig at the Sahara. As a favor to Prima, Miller booked him for a two-week stint—not as Prima had hoped in the hotel's main showroom, but at the pocket-sized stage

above: The Mary Kaye Trio pioneered the Vegas lounge act at the Last Frontier by performing on a small stage behind the bar near the casino floor.

right: Louis Prima and Keely Smith with Sam Butera and the Witnesses brought the lounge act to another level starting in 1954 at the Sahara's Casbar Lounge.

behind the casino bar at the Casbar lounge. Here's what the November 27, 1954 issue of *Jack Cortez' Fabulous Las Vegas Magazine* had to say about the act during its first week at the Casbar:

> We never saw the Casbar Lounge, in the Hotel Sahara, so jam-packed every night at every performance to early a.m., as we have this past week. The reason, LOUIS PRIMA, His Quintette, and his beautiful wife, KEELY SMITH, are the star attractions. Each performance, they present, will keep you glued to your seat, thrilled, and you automatically chalk up a tremendously great show. The superb and impromptu entertainment, plus Louis' inimitable song stylings, his "fooling around" with Keely is entertainment without par. Oh yes! Congratulations are also in order for the Primas, they are expecting a "Prima or Prima Donna" sometime in March!

Said Keely Smith in 1999, "Bill Miller had hired us for two weeks, and we stayed six years!" During their incredible run, Louis and Keely solidified the lounge act as quintessentially Las Vegas.

LAS VEGAS AFTER DARK | 97

opposite: Freddie Bell (second from left) and his Bell Boys at the Sands lounge was a high-energy act.

right: Twisting with sax legend Vido Musso.

left: Grooving to the sweet sounds of the accordion.

below: All barstools are fully occupied at the Fremont's Carnival Room lounge.

Liberace and Elvis ham it up in 1956. It was Elvis's first time performing in Las Vegas.

LAS VEGAS SHOWGIRLS

One of the most recognizable icons of the era was the Vegas showgirl with her voluptuous body (often appearing topless), feathery bejeweled costumes, fantastically towering headpieces, and elaborately choreographed stage routines. The midcentury incarnation of this type of showgirl had its origins in the 1920s' and '30s' New York burlesque shows of Florenz Ziegfeld, Earl Carroll, and the Minsky brothers. But it was in Havana, Cuba, during the island's spectacular postwar tourist boom that designer/director/choreographer Roderico Neyra (aka Rodney) perfected the themed musical stage show starring scantily clad dancers at the world's largest nightclub at the time, the Tropicana.

left: Quite a balancing act for this Desert Inn showgirl.

above: Vegas's fabulous shows and showgirls were the progeny of the elaborate early '50s productions of the Tropicana nightclub in Havana, Cuba.

right: A sultan's harem.

102 | GREETINGS FROM *Las Vegas*

In Las Vegas, these elaborate themed shows were mainstays of hotels such as the Stardust, with Donn Arden's long-running *Lido de Paris*, the Dunes with its *Casino de Paris*, and the Tropicana's *Folies Bergere* (hmmm, is there a theme here?). Even some of New York's famous showmen brought their productions to Las Vegas. Lou Walters's *Latin Quarter Revue* appeared up and down the Strip. The Minsky brothers' *Minsky's Follies* at the Desert Inn was the first Las Vegas revue to feature topless dancers. And then there were the famous solo burlesque performers who set up shop in the desert, the most famous of whom was Miss Lili St. Cyr, whose engagement at the El Rancho Vegas lasted for years.

left: A headdress designed by Freddie Krueger.

bottom right: Lili St. Cyr had a fashion model's figure and comportment. As a trained dancer, St. Cyr dazzled audiences in Las Vegas with her performing talent, expensive sets, and elaborate costumes. Her act was strictly "high class."

Glittery, talented, leggy, good-looking girls... a superb part of the nightly spectacle while you're dining in the beautiful Congo Room.

above: A headdress designed by Fred Rogers.

right: Miss Showgirl International 1969.

above: Margot desperate to recoup her massive losses at the Tropicana. "Baby needs shoes!"

above: Getting a kick watching Mrs. Hinkle miss 33 black, again.

right: "Craps, the most exciting game in the casino. There's excitement and anticipation with every roll of the dice."

CLASSIC LAS VEGAS RESTAURANTS

For many, indulging in continental-style fine dining at the big hotel-casinos was part of the Las Vegas experience. Each hotel had its own high-end restaurant, which added a note of elegance to contrast with the flashy casino floor nearby. Some of the more famous were the Sultan's Table at the Dunes, the Riviera's Hickory Room, the Painted Desert Room at the Desert Inn, the Sahara's House of Lords, the Candlelight Room at the Flamingo, and in the mid-1960s the Bacchanal at Caesars Palace.

The key elements of a classic fine-dining restaurant were white tablecloths, semicircular leather or vinyl booths in red, dark brown, or black, indirect lighting in dimly lit rooms, tuxedoed captains and waiters, and tableside service. Many featured dark wood paneling reminiscent of old-world European restaurants. Most of the Strip's fine-dining establishments lasted into the 1990s, finally disappearing one by one with the implosion of the Dunes, Sands, Desert Inn, and Stardust.

facing: Lovin' life at the Sahara's Congo Room in 1957.

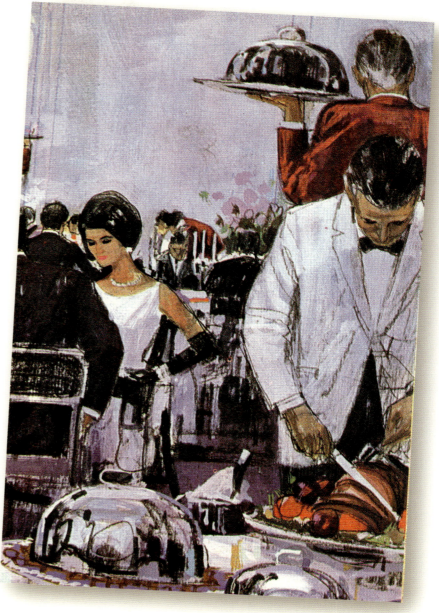

above:
Continental-style fine dining with tableside service at the Sahara's House of Lords.

LAS VEGAS AFTER DARK | 109

The Rat Pack

Although the group called itself "the Summit," the media and public knew them as the Rat Pack—Frank Sinatra, Dean Martin, Sammy Davis Jr., Peter Lawford, and Joey Bishop, among others. During the filming of *Ocean's 11* in 1960, the Rat Pack appeared nightly on the Sands's Copa Room stage, cracking each other up until the wee hours of the morning. They also acted together in two other films, *Sergeants 3* and *Robin and the 7 Hoods* (with Bing Crosby replacing a blackballed Lawford). Audiences loved the impromptu Sands performances, including numerous celebrities who crowded the front rows. Even after the group went its separate ways, Las Vegas in the early '60s would forever be known as the Rat Pack era.

facing: Frank Sinatra, Peter Lawford, and Dean Martin planning their heist in *Ocean's 11* near the Sahara's plaster camels.

right: The filming of *Ocean's 11* brought the Rat Pack to Las Vegas in 1960.

facing: On the Sands Copa stage in February 1960. From left, Dean Martin, Sammy Davis Jr., Peter Lawford, Frank Sinatra, Buddy Lester, Joey Bishop.

below: Dino in the Sands Copa Room. Jack Benny and Lucille Ball are in the front rows.

above: Frank Sinatra made the Sands the capital of cool.

left: Las Vegas lounge legend Buddy Greco, a jazz and pop singer and pianist, was a close friend of Frank Sinatra and an honorary member of the Rat Pack.

right: For Dean Martin's 1964 movie *Kiss Me, Stupid*, a neon caricature of Dino was temporarily added to the Sands marquee.

Sammy wows them in his sharkskin suit.

The Beautiful YUCCA MOTEL, 1727 SO. FIFTH ST., LAS VEGAS, NEV

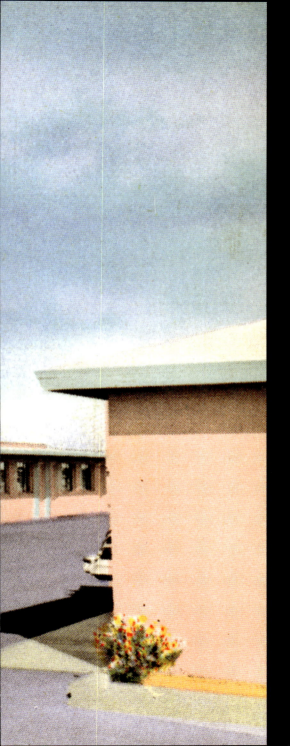

Motel Paradise

BY JERRY STEFANI

In the 1930s, with Boulder Dam bringing more tourists to Las Vegas by motorcar, auto courts were built with cabins surrounded by well-kept grounds. These were commonly located on Highway 91 (better known as Las Vegas Boulevard) near the center of the city's growth, Fremont Street. The majority of these auto courts were mom-and-pop operations with the duo living adjacent to the office near the street.

With Las Vegas gaining in popularity as a vacation destination after World War II, the motel offered just what Mom, Dad, and the kids were looking for—affordable luxury. The Las Vegas motel was the perfect cross between a cheap tourist cabin and a glamorous but pricey high-end hotel. With the passage of the Federal-Aid Highway Act in 1956, new freeways were built across the country, including Interstate 15 through Las Vegas, making the city even more accessible to motorists.

facing: On the Famous Strip of Las Vegas.

Jerry Stefani has been documenting Las Vegas's motel architecture since the 1980s. Growing up in California, Stefani spent much time in Las Vegas during visits with his father, a nuclear engineer who worked at the nearby Nevada Test Site. Jerry's "Las Vegas (and Reno) Motels—Then and Now" at StefaniDrivesVegas.com is the culmination of his exhaustive research.

The Home Motel offered a modest home away from home.

Cal-Neva Auto Court reflected an early form of vacationing by motorcar.

Full tiled showers, custom-built box springs and mattresses, and down pillows.

M.D. Close's Desert Rose Motel in 1953.

118 | GREETINGS FROM *Las Vegas*

Grandpa and Grandma taking a motel rest break on their way to Las Vegas in 1967.

MOTEL PARADISE | 119

above: Colorful Fremont Street motel with "Cribs & Sitter." Later known as Lucky Cuss Motel.

RADIO! POOL! TV! COLOR TV!

Pools were an important luxury that most motels were forced to afford. Then, starting in the mid-1950s, television became, by far, the single most important amenity motels could offer. Many Americans didn't own TVs in the 1950s, and the chance to spend a private evening with Lucy and Desi was a big draw for motels. FREE TV! the signs said. In the 1960s, COLOR TV performed the same function.

By the end of the 1950s, newer motels appeared south of Fremont Street on Las Vegas Boulevard all the way to the city limit at what is now Sahara Avenue. At the same time, motels continued to be built east on Fremont Street (also known as the Boulder Highway) all the way to—and beyond—Charleston Boulevard, and on the south end of Las Vegas Boulevard (the Strip) near McCarran Airport. According to the Las Vegas telephone directory, there were over 200 motels in the area by 1960.

right: Betty Willis designed the statuesque Blue Angel atop the motel of the same name. Willis is best known for designing the iconic "Welcome to Fabulous Las Vegas" sign.

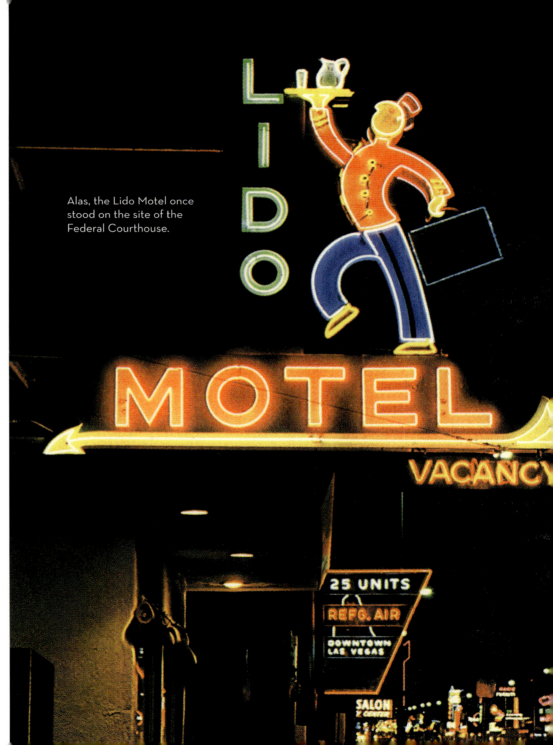

Alas, the Lido Motel once stood on the site of the Federal Courthouse.

As with most signage in Las Vegas, motel signs grew ever larger, achieving their most monumental street presence in the 1960s, especially for those located on the heart of the Strip. Soon, however, the mom-and-pop motels started to lose business as the national chains expanded. Guests were now seeking more amenities and consistency from accommodations. And chain motels were bigger, with expansive lobbies and interior access to guest rooms, indoor pools, recreation areas, and restaurants. They had national advertising, adorable mascots, and catchy slogans like "The best surprise is no surprise." Mostly they were clean with consistent quality and service. Chain motel pioneer Holiday Inn was founded in Memphis, Tennessee, in 1952, and quickly began franchising their system nationwide. Other chains such as Travelodge, Imperial 400, Best Western, and Motel 6 were all represented in Las Vegas.

left: Could you possibly cram more information on a motel sign?

below: Named after the famous city-state on the French Riviera.

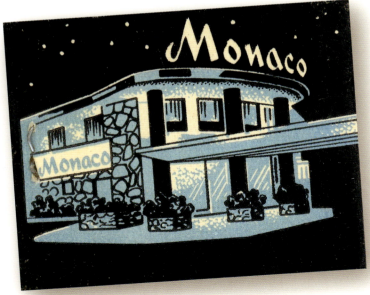

above, left: A motel that captures the spirit of Las Vegas.

above, right: TOD Motor Motel. A 1960s space-age beauty "Across the street from wedding chapel."

right: National chains such as TraveLodge slowly wiped out the mom-and-pop motels before being replaced themselves by megaresorts.

Few cities in America were ever blessed with as many mom-and-pop motel proprietors leaving the light on for travelers as was Las Vegas in the midcentury. For me, encountering a midcentury motel with its original neon sign and low-slung buildings along a highway in Las Vegas, or anywhere in America, remains profoundly inspiring.

below: Pioneering African American architect Paul R. Williams designed the Googie-style La Concha Motel in 1961. Located on the Strip just south of the Riviera, it closed in 2003. Miraculously, the lobby was saved and relocated as the new visitor's center for the must-see Neon Museum.

124 | GREETINGS FROM *Las Vegas*

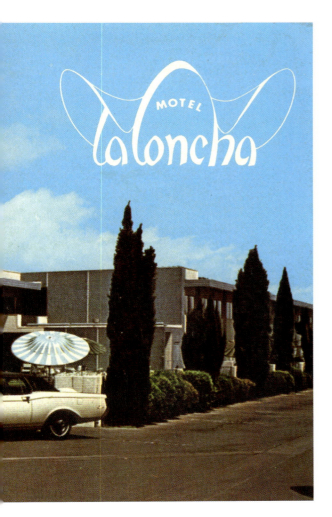

above: This spectacular resin-and-mosaic masterpiece graced the lobby behind the front desk.

left: There were no non-smoking rooms back in the day.

MOTEL PARADISE | 125

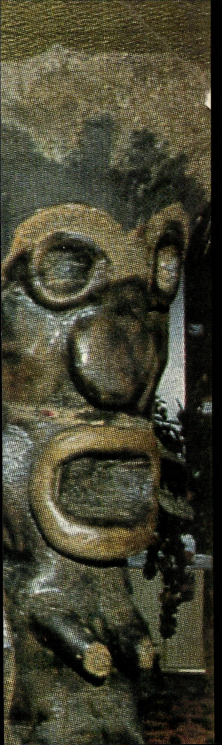

left: Big hair and big sideburns at the Stardust's Aku Aku

Tiki Vegas

BY SVEN A. KIRSTEN

Being as it was a city of fantasy, the imaginary world of Tiki seemed a good fit for Las Vegas. If an artificial oasis could rise out of the arid desert, why not an artificial South Sea island? Beginning with the Western Ranch look of early Vegas, a plethora of themed environments had evolved by the 1960s offering a variety of choices to entertainment-hungry visitors. Polynesian Tiki style was one of many escapist concepts in a cityscape populated with sultans, clowns, Romans, and cowboys.

And so, the giant Easter Island heads of the Aku Aku restaurant rose up next to the space-age glamour of the cosmic Stardust sign—a fitting union, since midcentury Tiki style worked best in contrast to jet age Modernism. In establishing a flavor and feeling of authenticity, no expense

Originally hailing from the German port town of Hamburg, Sven Kirsten decided to make California his home at age 25. While he continued to pursue his career as a director of photography in Los Angeles, his visual sense led him to appreciate American midcentury architecture and design, particularly the uncharted field of Tiki. After four books, several exhibitions, and countless lectures on Tiki style, Sven has emerged as the country's singular authority on the subject.

was spared at the Aku Aku. Polynesian pop veteran Donn Beach—Don the Beachcomber himself—and Edward Brownlee, an authority on South Pacific artifacts, were flown in from Waikiki to work on the project. The giant stone gods by the A-frame entrance and the roadside sign were chiseled by Eli Hedley from volcanic rock.

left: Lei ceremony for the Aku Aku's Easter Island mascot.

above: A taste of Polynesia on the Las Vegas Strip.

right: Like most Polynesian bars and restaurants, the Aku Aku had its own ceramic Tiki mug.

130 | GREETINGS FROM *Las Vegas*

After such deep-concept decor, it seems strange that the next Polynesian palace of note—the actual namesake of Don the Beachcomber at the Sahara—was anything but authentic. While it featured the customary waterways and some Polynesian murals (with a few Tikis from Whittier, California, supplier Oceanic Arts thrown in), the overwhelming impression of the space was one of *I Dream of Jeannie*. The purple floor-to-ceiling color scheme was punctuated by white gazebos with a stylized palm-leaf pattern; and instead of glass floats as hanging lamps, brassy chandeliers completed the room's Eleganza look. Clearly, the Sahara's version of the Don the Beachcomber brand had wandered far from then-established classic Tiki style.

right: Don the Beachcomber was a prominent addition to the Sahara in 1962.

below: Soft pastels and sleek mahogany form a tastefully subdued atmosphere in the bar area.

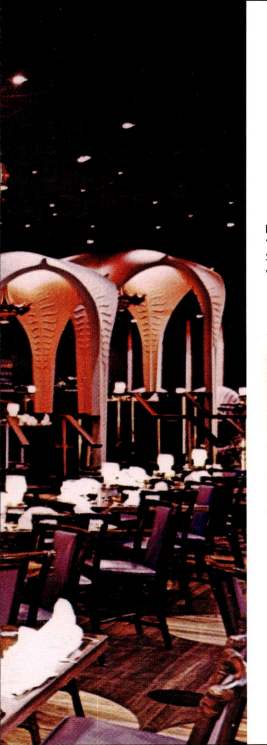

left: The surreal pod-like "individual dining huts" of the Sahara's Don the Beachcomber were a bit disturbing.

right: A rare Sahara tiki mug featuring Don the Beachcomber himself.

TIKI VEGAS | 133

Another place promising "South Seas island living" was the Castaways, across from the Sands. Inspired by the lavish Miami Beach resort of the same name, its design was more Exotica Moderne than Polynesian. Perusing photographs of the Samoa Room theater and the Kon Tiki Lounge reveal precious few Tiki touches amongst the Vegas vinyl and brass. Its main attraction, the Gateway to Luck, was a hand-carved, life-sized replica of a Jain temple—exotic, but not exactly what you would find as a castaway on a South Sea island.

above: The Castaways was more Exotica Moderne than Polynesian.

left: The "I Dream of Jeannie" suite. The bar is sheltered by a flying carpet. Hanging beads disguise the bedroom.

right: Nothing screams "exotic" like a stack of colored balls.

134 | GREETINGS FROM *Las Vegas*

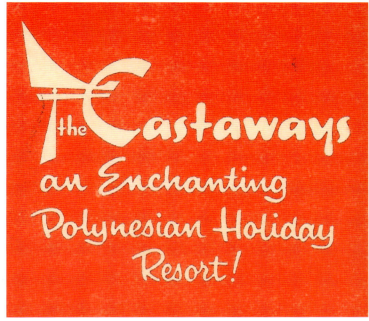

TIKI VEGAS | 135

It is regrettable then that Steve Crane's Luau Room at the Royal Nevada, which was rendered in painstaking detail in classic Tiki style by the design team of Clif and Lou Sawyer, only lasted a few years in the late 1950s. It seems Las Vegas wanted to interpret the Tiki style in its own way and did so—sometimes successfully, sometimes not.

left: Painstakingly rendered interior for the Royal Nevada's short-lived Luau Room.

below: Nothing was exotic about this motel but its name.

TIKI VEGAS | 137

Vegas Modern

Almost all of the architects working in Las Vegas after World War II were fluent in Modernism. When given the chance they would produce buildings of rigor, sophistication, and beauty. Alan Hess's seminal *Viva Las Vegas: After-Hours Architecture* of 1993 is the key reference book that explores the origins, influences, evolution, and importance of Las Vegas's commercial architecture and its designers.

One of the first master architects to bring his skills to the desert was George Vernon Russell. With the Flamingo Hotel project of 1945–46, Russell's task was to bring the glamour of the swank nightclubs he designed on Los Angeles's

facing: Wayne McAllister's Sands of 1952 was a modern, sculptural tour de force.

Sunset Strip to Las Vegas. Despite, or because of, the involvement of Benjamin "Bugsy" Siegel, he succeeded.

Wayne McAllister was a Los Angeles–based architect who applied the Late Moderne commercial style to the Sands in 1952, with a special emphasis on the building's porte cochere and front entrance. On the west side of the glazed doors were vertical fins with brushed aluminum bezel frames featuring coming attractions; a dazzling marble wall was on the opposite side. The freestanding roadside sign was an extension of the architecture, with its eggcrate grid projecting from and above a soaring pylon.

To keep up with design trends, in 1953 the six-year-old Flamingo was completely remodeled by the architectural firm of Pereira and Luckman, also of Los Angeles. An upswept flat roof floated over a row of delicate illuminated cylinders. A wall of sparkling glass fronted the main entrance. And presiding over the composition was a champagne tower of rising neon bubbles topped by a rotating Flamingo sign.

above: Architect George Vernon Russell brought the sophistication of the Sunset Strip nightclubs he designed to the desert.

below: The 1952 Sahara was influenced by the low-slung Ranch Modern houses popular in Southern California, but with the addition of a prominent porte cochere.

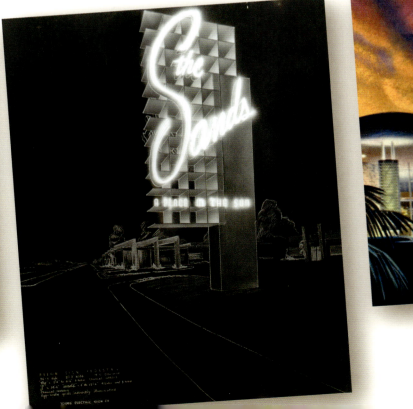

140 | GREETINGS FROM *Las Vegas*

above: A kidney-shaped sign next to the clean horizontal lines and ribbon windows of the façade. Miami Modern meets the International style.

facing: Fabricated by YESCO, Wayne McAllister's Sands sign was a monumental work of art linked architecturally to the building.

above: The luminous 1953 remodel of the Flamingo at dusk.

above: Rising majestically from the center of Old West–themed Glitter Gulch, the 1956 Fremont Hotel by Wayne McAllister and William Wagner was a monument to Midcentury Modernism. Hotel rooms in a vertical slab of interlocking concrete panels rest on a wide platform containing a casino, showroom, pool, and restaurants.

VEGAS MODERN | 141

In Las Vegas's postwar residential neighborhoods some of the new tract developments were as modern in design as the resorts being built on the Strip. Architect William Krisel, of the Los Angeles firm Palmer and Krisel, was the design architect behind the Paradise Palms tract surrounding the Stardust Golf Club. Paradise Palms offered dozens of different floor plans, roof shapes, and exterior concrete block decorative patterns to choose from. The Beverly Green neighborhood northeast of the Strip is another pocket

MODEL 7A

MODEL 7B

MODEL 7C

left: Three of architect William Krisel's modern house models for the Paradise Palms tract.

above: The circular fireplace in the center of Wilbur Clark's mod living room features a conical hood, natural rock border, and travertine marble seating area. It was one of the fabulous custom homes built in Clark's Desert Inn Estates development on the resort's golf course.

of original Midcentury Modern houses. Wilbur Clark's Desert Inn Estates, since demolished, contained many extraordinary Modern residences by local architect Hugh Taylor. Rancho Nevada Estates contains a mix of custom Ranch Modern and Desert Modern houses on half-acre lots. And scattered throughout Las Vegas within a mile or two of the Strip are 1950s and 1960s neighborhoods of Modern custom and tract houses such as McNeil Estates, Glen Heather Estates, and Desert Park.

right: Wilbur Clark turns a knob on his overly complicated yet clearly impressive built-in, high-tech entertainment system.

VEGAS MODERN | 143

above: The Paradise Palms flat roof model with glass walls facing the backyard pool.

facing: One of the rare split-level homes in Paradise Palms. Concrete screen block successfully used for dramatic effect.

The desert's last prospector contemplates Las Vegas's futuristic new convention center and the thousands of conventioneers who would descend—apparently by helicopter—to mix business and pleasure at nearby hotels.

Through the '50s and '60s, the Strip hotels continued to remodel and expand, abandoning the Old West theme for up-to-date Modernism utilizing a variety of midcentury architectural influences: jet age, space age, International style, Neo-Expressionism, New Formalism, and Corporate Modernism. The Last Frontier became the New Frontier, the Las Vegas Convention Center and Landmark Hotel landed east of the Strip, McCarran Airport was upgraded, and the new Dunes tower outshone its rivals in ultramodern style.

above: In the early 1960s, the Los Angeles–based firm Welton Becket and Associates designed new facilities for McCarran Airport, including a terminal similar to Eero Saarinen's Neo-Expressionist TWA terminal at JFK built around the same time.
left: Designed by Chicago-based architect Milton M. Schwartz, the Dunes's new 1964 addition was called "the Diamond of the Dunes." It would be the most ultramodern hotel ever erected in the desert.
right: The Landmark Hotel, its prickly flying saucer atop an octagonal shaft.

VEGAS MODERN | 147

With the Melvin Grossman–designed Caesars Palace of 1966, the classical architecture of Imperial Rome was reinterpreted in the style of New Formalism. As described by Alan Hess, the resort's Corinthian columns were "abstracted as fluid, tapering stems melting into arches." Between the arches and covering the hotel's facade were Moorish-style patterned screens of concrete block.

Unfortunately, starting in the 1970s, Las Vegas's exuberant postwar design experimentation devolved into the bland Modernism of corporate America. It would be decades before the vibrant, high-Modernism of CityCenter would bring cutting-edge architecture back to Las Vegas.

left: The classical architecture of Imperial Rome reinterpreted in the style of New Formalism at Caesars Palace.

below: Bland corporate modernism became the norm starting in the 1970s.

VEGAS MODERN | 149

Popular Modernism found its greatest expression in the Googie style, applied to coffee shops, supermarkets, car washes, automobile showrooms, bowling centers, and a wide variety of retail stores. Googie, named after the Sunset Boulevard coffee shop Googies in Los Angeles, where the style first appeared, featured exaggerated and often colorful architectural elements combined with large neon-lit signage to draw the attention of speeding motorists. In addition, the ability to "bring the outdoors in" made possible through the technology of floor-to-ceiling plate glass windows was a typical Googie design feature. In the late '50s and early '60s, jet age elements such as uplifted or tilting rooflines were particularly emphasized. The Googie style was applied to many Las Vegas buildings, such as restaurants, an automobile showroom, and especially motels.

facing: The rocket supporting the Findlay Oldsmobile sign sets the theme for the auto showroom, with glass walls barely restraining the roof from soaring into space. **above:** The main building of the 1964 El Morocco Motel looked like a world's fair pavilion, entirely round with a ring of deeply scalloped windows enlivening its facade. **right, center:** The office for the 3 Coins Motel featured a jet age hyperbolic paraboloid roof. **right:** Multicolored rocks accentuate the soaring roof sheltering the Alpine Village Inn, famous for "Unique Dining."

VEGAS MODERN | 151

Renowned African American architect Paul R. Williams designed the Neo-Expressionist La Concha Motel of 1961 (above) and the 1963 A-frame Guardian Angel Cathedral (left).

152 | GREETINGS FROM *Las Vegas*

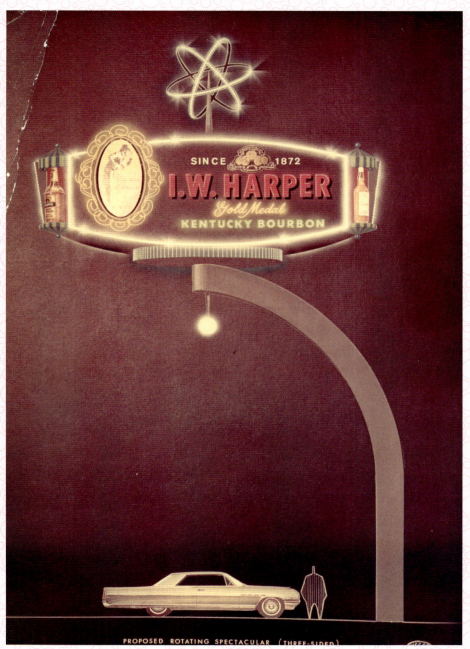

right: It's doubtful that this towering, atomic-powered, space age "proposed rotating spectacular" of bourbon was actually erected.

VEGAS MODERN | 153

Swinging '60s and Beyond

In the late 1950s, Las Vegas suffered an economic downturn as the tropical holiday destinations of Miami Beach and Havana reached their apex of popularity. In Miami Beach, high-rise hotels like the Fontainebleau, Eden Roc, Americana, Saxony, and Carillon had many more rooms than perhaps any Las Vegas hotel did at the time. Miami Beach was also closer to the northeastern population centers and easier to reach than Las Vegas. In addition, Havana—a short one-hour flight from Miami—had recently welcomed a trio of big, modern hotel-casinos with Santo Trafficante's Capri, the Habana Hilton, and Meyer Lansky's Riviera opening between 1956 and 1958. It seemed that many high rollers were choosing the diverse pleasures of the "Paris of the Caribbean" over Nevada's remote desert resort.

The tide turned in 1959–60, when Castro's revolution effectively shut down the island's casinos to the

facing: Miss Buttercup and her T-Bird friends.

immediate benefit of Las Vegas. Miami Beach continued to thrive for a few more years until the late 1960s, when its glossy sheen began to fade. Meanwhile, Las Vegas in the 1960s saw the completion of Caesars Palace, Circus Circus, the Landmark, and high-rise expansions of the Sahara, Dunes, Flamingo, and Sands. The year 1969 was especially momentous, with the opening of the massive International (one of the world's largest hotels upon completion), which hosted the triumphant return of Elvis to Las Vegas that year.

far left: Miami Beach was America's top resort going into the 1960s.

left: Havana was strong competition for Las Vegas when lavish hotels such as Meyer Lansky's Havana Riviera opened in the late 1950s.

above: A towering sultan greets guests to the original Dunes of 1955.

left: The first major expansion of the Dunes in 1961 included the Sultan's Table fine-dining restaurant and a convention hall.

above: The ultramodern Diamond of the Dunes tower of 1964 contrasts sharply with the kitschy rooftop sultan, who would soon retire to the sign boneyard on the edge of town.

right: The Dunes Top O' the Strip. "Providing a breathtaking view of the most fabulous city on Earth—Las Vegas!"

SWINGING '60S AND BEYOND | 157

THE DUNES DOME OF THE SEA

There have been many fantastically themed motels, hotels, and restaurants constructed in Las Vegas, but none have been as over-the-top fabulous as the Dome of the Sea at the Dunes. Following the demolition of the original hotel in 1963, the Dome of the Sea was built where the sultan statue had once stood guard. Architect Milton F. Schwartz was especially proud of the seafood restaurant, saying of its unusual form in a 2005 interview, "The Dome of the Sea was something I had always wanted to design. It was a circular building and it looked like it came from outer space. It just felt like it fit on the desert to me." Amen.

According to Schwartz, "The restaurant was called the Dome of the Sea because it was meant to be a seafood restaurant. I had chosen a woman with long, golden blond hair. She was five-foot-six and played a harp, a golden harp, and I placed her in a seashell in the center of the restaurant that rolled around on a figure-eight track in the water. She would play the harp in this seafood restaurant in the water. Not in the water—but she sat in the seashell and the seashell-shaped seat. The people were mesmerized by the music and the ambiance of the restaurant; it was very beautiful." And weird in a very, very good way.

Dome of the Sea

left: A golden maiden strums her harp while her seashell perch makes a figure eight in this shimmering nautical world.

right: This beautiful menu is made of a plastic mesh that gives the appearance of shimmering water.

Dome of the Sea

DUNES HOTEL AND COUNTRY CLUB, LAS VEGAS, NEVADA

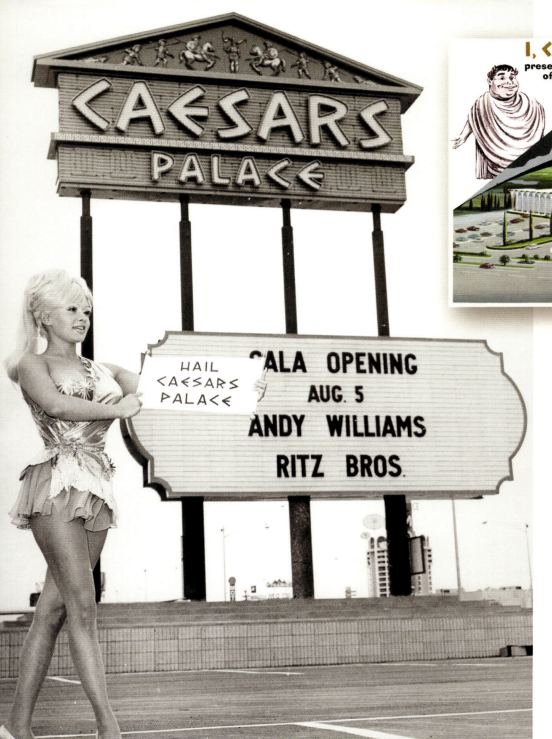

above: The opulence and grandeur of Imperial Rome was the theme of the 1966 Caesars Palace. Caesars would be the prototype for the themed megaresorts of the 1990s and 2000s that Steve Wynn and others perfected.

left: "Hail Caesars Palace," indeed.

facing: The new International was the site of Elvis Presley's triumphant return to Las Vegas in 1969, inaugurating a new phase of his career.

SWINGING '60S AND BEYOND | 161

left: The Sands built its scalloped circular tower in 1965. **above:** A flying saucer crowned the pie-shaped rooms of the Landmark Hotel. Financial problems caused an eight-year delay in its 1969 opening, seen here amidst the glamour of Las Vegas just off the Strip. **below:** The subtle touch of fuchsia was the pièce de résistance of the 777 redecorated guest rooms. **facing:** At 2,200 rooms, the MGM Grand became the world's largest hotel when it opened in 1973. It suffered a deadly fire in 1980.

SWINGING '60S AND BEYOND | 163

left: At the Tropicana, one waits for Madame.

below: The north end of the Strip in 1965.

left: Tom makes an important sales call while waiting for Madame.

below left: Tom, relaxing with the guys.

below: A disgarded concept painting for a Sahara facelift.

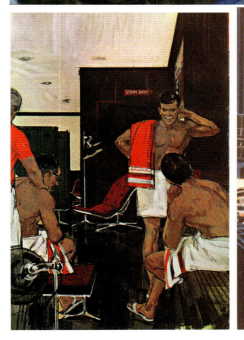

SWINGING '60S AND BEYOND | 165

facing: Elvis shows off to Ann-Margret in the 1964 classic *Viva Las Vegas*.

above: Tropicana showgirls of the Folies Bergere.

right: A 1970s view looking east from the Union Plaza Hotel pool, which floats above Fremont Street.

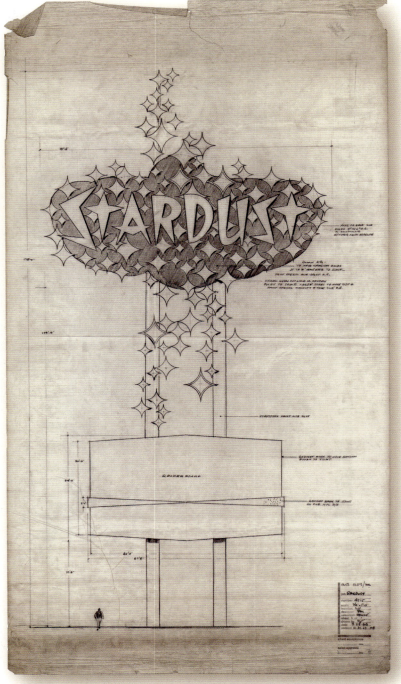

168 | GREETINGS FROM *Las Vegas*

facing far left: The famous 1958 outer-space Stardust facade was replaced with one of the greatest roadside signs ever built. This 1966 drawing by Ad Art Sign Co. depicts its final form.

facing above: The gargantuan size of the new Stardust sign dwarfs the men below.

facing below: Putting it all together.

above: The Stardust sign towers above the plethora of signage in 1977.

right: The prestigious *Art in America* magazine examines the significance of the Stardust sign in 1972.

170 | GREETINGS FROM *Las Vegas*

facing: Fremont Street pulsates with energy in 1969.

above: Under Del Webb's ownership, The Mint replaced its cool undulating sidewalk canopy with something horizontal and boring.

SWINGING '60S AND BEYOND | 171

facing: Benny Binion's Horseshoe casino inaugurated the World Series of Poker in 1970. Here, in 1976, Doyle Brunson (the bald guy), known as "Texas Dolly," is about to win the tournament and $300,000.

right: The closest wedding chapel to the Clark County Courthouse was across the street. Parking in rear.

below: The south end of the Strip in 1970.

SWINGING '60S AND BEYOND | 173

The 1970s was the era of corporatization. Hilton bought the International and Flamingo. Holiday Inn and Ramada came to town. Existing hotels added more high-rises that were generally big, rectangular, and mirrored, like office buildings, indistinguishable from their neighbors. In the coming decades the small motels, gas stations, rental car agencies, and convenience stores wedged between resort properties vanished one by one. The pioneering hotel-casinos—the Frontier, Desert Inn, Sands, Dunes, Hacienda, Stardust, Castaways, Landmark, and Aladdin—were all imploded in sad, degrading spectacles. A few Fremont Street classics survive intact, such as Vegas Vic and Binion's. Miraculously, the original 1941 El Cortez with its 1952 neon signage is a stalwart survivor.

left: Flavorless corporate modernism of the 1970s Dunes.

below left: One of many implosions that decimated classic Las Vegas in recent decades, making room for the themed megaresorts of the Strip.

below right: Welcome to the 1980s.

facing: The original El Cortez of 1941 was listed in the National Register of Historic Places in 2013 for its architectural integrity and important role in the early growth of Fremont Street. The nomination was written and submitted by the author with the support of the owners.

above left: 1983. First visit to Las Vegas, age 21.

above center: 1992. With close friend Jerry Stefani. The Luxor rises in the background.

above right: 1995. In YESCO's boneyard.

right: 2014. Celebrating the author's successful nomination placing the El Cortez in the National Register of Historic Places.

Historian Peter Moruzzi was born in Concord, Massachusetts, and raised in Hawaii. He graduated from the University of California at Berkeley and later attended the American Film Institute in Los Angeles. In 1999, he founded the Palm Springs Modern Committee, an architectural preservation group. Moruzzi is the author of numerous pictorial histories, including *Palm Springs Holiday* and *Greetings from Los Angeles*.